The Lost Religion of Men

(All Bob Is Clemente)

CEE

Featured Model: Jessica Marie Barnes

Interior layout by Robert Louis Henry

Published by
Leaf Garden Press
LeafGardenPress.com

To the United States District Court for the Western District of Arkansas and Indian Territory, 1875-1891, as presided by Judge Isaac C. Parker

And

To a cleanshaven George Carlin, straw hat, striped jacket, group-singing "Winchester Cathedral" on *The Kraft Summer Music Hall*, 1966

I hope The Reader, takes my meaning...

"The past, though perhaps somewhat uncompleted, is mostly itself; the present is always zany and elusive; and the future, maybe, is a game of Roller Ball Murder."

—from the Preface to *Roller Ball Murder*,
a collection of short stories by William Harrison
(1974; William Morrow & Company, Inc.)

BOB

At some near point, humans live for the cliché. The long shot winner, the hooker with the heart of gold, the cavalry over the hill, guidon rippling. The tearful reconciliation. The son reported missing at Tarawa, who turns up grinning, at the door. Roy Hobbes, Not striking out. "You had me at 'hello'." New Frontier. Great Society. *"I have a dream!"* I have 'em too, Rev. They're usually caused by pizza.

Human creatures, putting "Zero" instead of "Diet" on a can, then talking Zig Ziglar, 78RPM, the FEDEX guy of my teens, "how it's Not the same". No. False. That uncreative, *is always exactly The Same*. And, once you get past the *faux*, New Age rebop, about Infinite Diversity in Infinite Combinations, every man, woman and child you will ever chance to meet—exception of a couple—will act like they came out if a spray can. Sameness, lockstep, change which is not, contrived to maintain/reestablish Order, are cattle prods for The Herd…as are lines of demarcation.

There's a certain OCD quality, to even The Law. I don't smoke, but if a 4th grader wants to go that far out of their way, *hey*, I've told you I'm no one's keeper. As for the other end, carding rickety people who hang with your grandparents, OMG, you're stupid. As is the anal retentive company you're kneeling to. Disobey, nonfriend. Do your Martin Luther of the Crullers, sue for wrongful dismissal, then be prepared to sit, talking head, on MSNBC and FOX. And, be prepared for the anal retentive position, to be defended like a piece of the One True Cross. Bogart-ing its default position. Nimbus at a jaunty angle.

Humans believe in fronted jars. They believe in endlessly spreading napkins. Mom believed I should be crucified for PLAYBOYs at 14, but the unspeakable stuff, at 18? *"Oh, well, you're old enough now, to make your own decisions…"* Really? How's 'bout I refuse to draw lines for purposes nonsensical? Like it was DIFFERENT, 2000, as opposed to 1999. No, it wasn't. You know what was different? *"Where in Hell did the VHS section go?!"* THAT'S what was different.

Social evolution doesn't occur on cue. It's generally forced by the nonapathetic, on all those drifting to Byzantium. This is happening, today, WhackaLaw. It happens, every now and then, it's nothing unusual. But, *c'mon.* Seriously. Using a change in the relative appearance of the *Anno Domini*, is kindergarten marketing, Playskool sociology. Malibu Stacey, with a new hat. Slap them paws together and honk at the number, Brosius. Thangs, they's *diff'runt! G'yuuuhh!*

That's how the Millennium was ushered in. And, it's how the 70s was ushered. Media, for their own purposes or They of the smoke-filled room, echoing Johnny Cochrane *cum South Park*, "Look at the monkey! Look at the silly monkey!"

I was cached at an older neighbor friend's, New Year's Eve, 1969. Across the street, thirty strides, from my Dad's. Dad was going out, and Mom going out, elsewhere, and in my little universe, I like to think their evenings consisted of penny poker and gossip. Perhaps a loud laugh, at a tale from someone's life. How Governor Ogilvie was a jerk. Or something. The opening martini go-'round in *The Graduate*, was not welcome. The rest of that movie, God killed you for.

I passed out early. I think. I couldn't hang. I vaguely remember The Ball, but it's (maybe?) because I awoke to relative noise of the ritual. "The Ball". Yay. Pink Floyd pig of Times Square...that's exciting...

The world in which I fell asleep, was Nixon, and it was hardhat. It was Billy Graham and *Faith For Today*. It was flowers and long hair. It was black fists, and bloody faces in camou. It was a mouth calling itself a boxer. It was "WAR", scraped cave, on lower STOP sign.

My world, TV aerial-heralded, was peacocks and Big Eyes. Johnny. Bob Hope, not funny, on Johnny. Ballplayers, hard of face, dating from the Cold War. Broadcasts of runny color, via satellites that worked half the time. Hubert Humphrey's nasal twang. Paul Lynde's nasal twang. Howard Cosell's nasal growl. Churches of Our Choice and ancient Chinese secrets. I had entered this world—relatively speaking, this world—in its post-dawn, with tanks in East Berlin. I had known no other. There was little of the bag shaken, since that time. Only the older kids, unable further, to keep any fluid or gas self-contained. I admit, I preferred the ones I'd known as a toddler, paintings with letter sweaters, two-tone convertibles, two-tone shoes.

That changed. Sure. The VHS tapes went away. Not much else. But, of course, now, here, when I awoke, it would be January 1·, 1970...and Buffalo Big Brother, would tell us things were different. We have always been at war with Tradition. We have always been at peace with Change. And The Herd, acting like one, would git 'long. Until crewcuts were mutton chop mops and "Bob" on your TOPPS Clemente's, looked strange, even to you...and the dawgies would continue *Wagon Train*-ing, until, bowling alley, barber shop, state fair, bar, only Midway's Golden Arm as artifact, remained. I thought it was arm wrestling machine. Competition. "You, versus". It wasn't. It was marketed, very clearly, as a "strength tester". It tested strength. I remember I used to see that everywhere, growing up. It doesn't exist, Today. Strength, I mean. Like Rhodes' Colossus, just a legend.

But, it didn't go away, in one day.

CEE,
braced for reentry against the
hatch cover of Liberty Bell 7,
July 21, 1961

Tribal Markings

weakling*
(local tough and beaten hippie, 1969)

Whenever you get up of a day, now,
go in the bathroom and
look in the mirror
look into your squinty, Jappo eyes
behind your loser, Dexter glasses
get a good look at the pits in your
craggy face
the doughy white of you
the oily hair with things living in it
your big lips
remember the things you do to yourself
every day,
because no woman worth anything will
do them for you
look at yourself
smell yourself
imagine yourself in twenty years
and then, think this and say it out loud:
"Men are bleeding out in rice paddies
All so's I get to be
'this'"

...I...I'm a man, too.

No, you're not
but, when you get your first period
gimme a call

> *—excerpted and converted from the CEE ghost story,
> "Black Happiness"

5

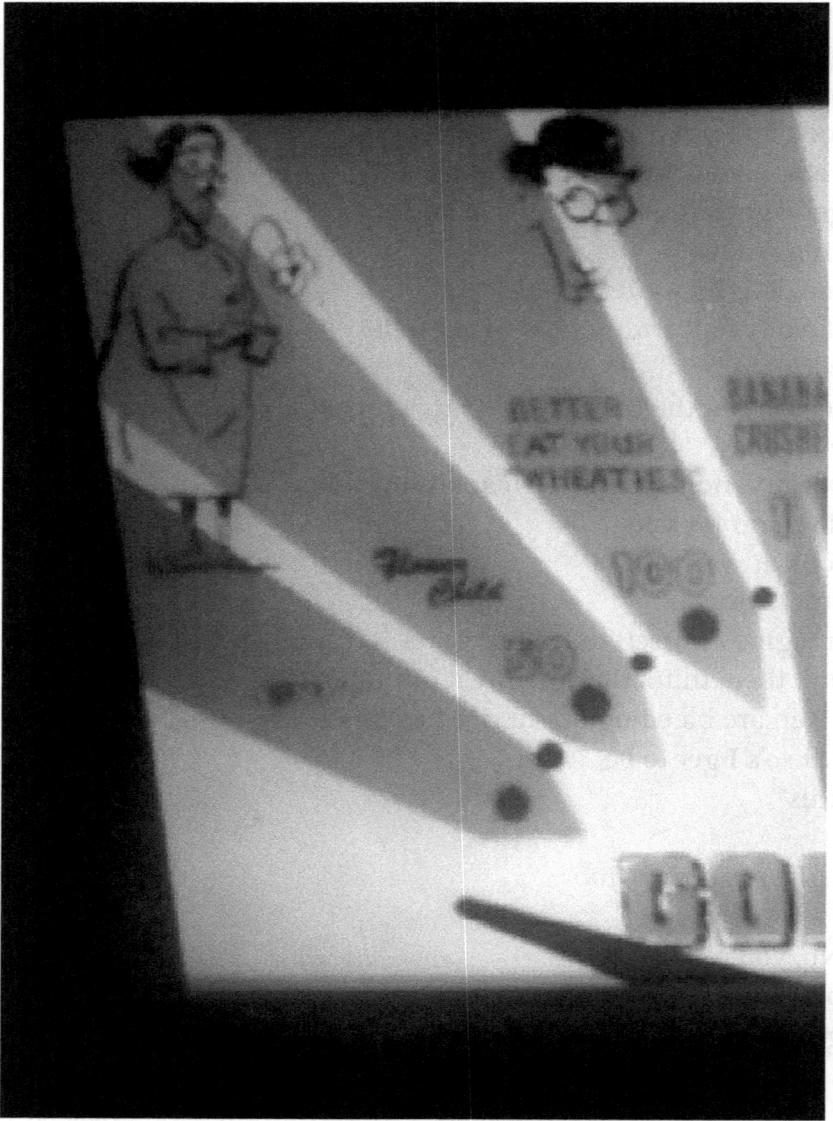

Flower's Child is Full of Shit (for Jasper Redd)

I have oft times wondered--
This is the truth--
Why Nixon hardhats
Didn't just kill them
Why The Guard, clear line if sight
Didn't operate WATCHMEN-world
And kill them
Why the average citizen
"obliging motorist" picking up hitchers
Why the angry dad   or mom!
Why the one professor who Disagreed
Why the local cops or local toughs
The neighbor or store owner
Who'd had enough
Had Marx and King and Dylan's
Sandpaper, I-smoke-unfiltered-Chesterfields
Wheezes
Right Up To 'Here'
Why another young person
Life Up Ahead
Didn't push chips, all in
Knowing this change could not be stopped
Knowing they could stop It There

So, there Are No "Haters", not Here
Not in my book
If you Hate, you kill what you hate
If you're suicidal, you kill yourSelf
Why did those barefoot, in The End
Wear Bruno Magli?
Well?
Why is the NYC skyline, so changed
These many years?

Well?

Why Washington Should Have Accepted a Crown
(March Nanners)

Your freedom means my enslavement
So, tough
Do something about it
This might mean your enslavement
But I will prevent You
From enslaving Me,
And we're butting heads eternally
Lazarus and Lazarus
In that one *Star Trek* episode
Yes
That's Life
It's a dynamic
All or nothing, Bill W.
Because my freedom is
I want you dead

You Marry One Person (spoiler alert!)

In observing random in-laws' treatment of
"the one They brought home"
Cold plexi existing between Outsider,
I find ritual of Other family, sad
Then, I hear what I've begged God to be
Apocryphal,
Usually, matriarch to Outsider "son",
Opening up a Mason jar of
Whoopimperiousness
As a general rule, that would mostly be
A lot of "ordering about",
Coming by way of the coldest
The most detached,
"I despise you with every fiber of my being"
Creature,
On the other side of the plexi;
I married late in Life, by then, a-tremble
Cash, ready to kill Douglas
Or Douglas, ready to go down trying to
Kill Cash
Over initial, "Who The Fuck, Are YOU?!"
(that, or this whole, "honeydew" bullshit...
nuhnuhnuh...one hires it done...
my Type A, war hero Pop knew That)
You might know, though,
I married into a peaceful family of pandas
Who aren't quite certain, the
Catamount in their midst
So, no one's in Hell or on Death Row
Which leaves me cold only if I quiet-think,
80's action flick falling action,
Of the ones who never made it to
Smurf's Village
Those millions outside the plexi
Who realize, and care that they're there

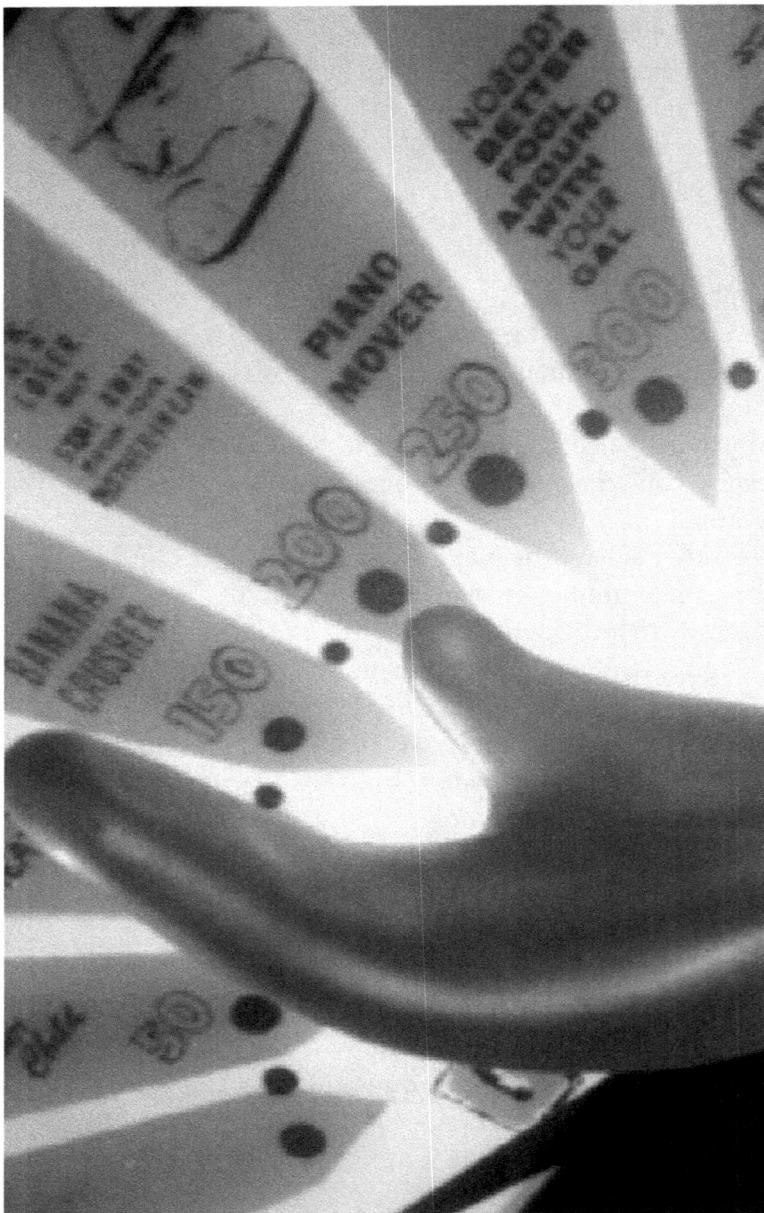

Like English Lords, laughing at Belfast

Fans of The Stooges
Can be downright snobbish
Right down to the #BOINK#
Then again, any devotees, y'know,
Bond fans who despise why You
Like/don't like 007,
Beer-drunk elder snotting, 1976
I dared compare Frampton to Clapton!
But, something's quintessential-y
"A wise guy, eh?"
Re: cloth napkin ruling class'
Victorian—ass guffaw at Moe—Victorian
Shift
Too WW2 Superman phone booth, for me
I wonder at object lesson of
Serious and frumpy, brutes, the
Obviously superior, the malevolent
The Wurmtung murder-eyed
Petty dens of charcoal-smear beard thugs
The shorts' version of Tor Johnson
Or a monster,
Thwarted by accidents *ex machinae*
Divine timing and the absurd
All the while, angry, demented lessers
Jack Bauer-ing one another with
Directed tortures
Before running triad, Jims Thorpe,
Down Lombard St., after escaped piano,
Which, given our culture, 80, 90 years ago,
Might have killed someone as normal
"We're filming, officer!"
"Oh…all right…"
…which, I s'pose, though stereo, explains
Their fans this minute, snorting into their
Hand-dipped Mozartkugeln

"Alpha"
(Gamma-alpha-mu-alpha sigma-alpha-sigma)

And, I blow the tight-jawed SOB
Into the street, dead
No, I'm a crazy asshole
Default: COP
And, I brain the humanimal
With a semi-pro bat, keep swinging
No, I'm a psycho
COP
I kick his ass in the parking lot
Of a gangland watering hole
But don't stop at first blood, bowed head
No mumble-sorry, crummy Eastwood
No, I'm a dangerous thing
COP (at least one, lazy, raising questions)
There isn't any Defeating The Myth
Of evo-psych lie creature
You can't rend him from his bestseller
"I read to be a man, I larn it from a booook"
You just have to be silent
Allow fake WBA belt to grace
Fake champ's whatheis
Figuring, hoping
He's one of 'em who goes to a supermax
Rape-rape, rape-itty raperape,
Because he killed his Her, anyway
Or he's one looking wise and hormone
Her, too, and proud
About all the erections that are really
Dishwashing

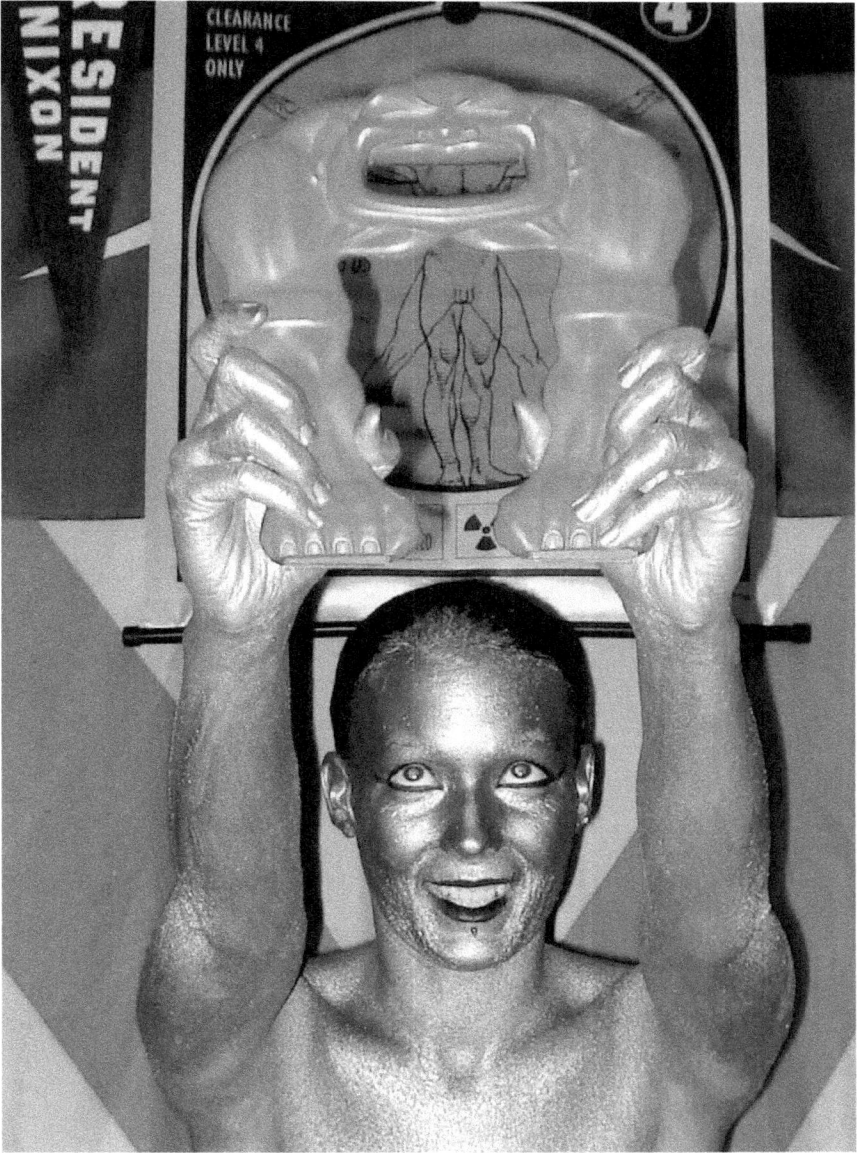

Spanning the tickticktick...

Johnny U. Are There

Life as America as purpose itself
Manufactured logic as made sense
Johnny U., with a crewcut Matt Groening
Could set his 90s punchline by
If there exist no other distractions, well
You might be in your fat cousin's bedroom
You're blowing bubble gum
That cut your cheek
Before you softened it
There's a gun rack on the wall
Beyond that, TV aerial, high sky
Past there, muddy fields strewn of chaff
The harvest came, the land is sleeping
Parents are taking care of things
and the police
and the governor
and the folks on Capitol Hill
all in hand   all is good
Red Soviets or no, We Are Right
Those who dissent are dirty folk,
There is beauty in simplicity
The last moment we children of Iwo Jima,
Would Ever be defined by our
Responsibilities
a future for us, a nation for us
world enough and Time...and on Sundays,
Johnny Unitas, already growing old, fading back,
kicking ass in a man's game meant for men
Leader. General. Star. Magicks away, long bomb
All found talisman through show glass,
In a TOPPS football card priced at
Too-Much.95

Smoke Army (My, Oh, My)

"I don't think I can watch
Anymore of this, son,"
Says Mom, as a meat cleaver
Staves in Jerry Quarry's head
"Why?" queries outrage of Youth
Outraged, as a
Lead pipe caves in Quarry's ribs
"Mom, we watch boxing
All the time!"
"Not like this," tiny words, small micro
As a brick bat crushes Quarry's face,
"Aww, whaddaya mean?!"
Shocked, head swiveling
Missing Quarry's head being taken
Clean away,
"Son," Mom says, for real frightened
Spellbound at Patton tank rolling over
Jerry Quarry,
"It's this *Frazier!* Son, he's a *Killer!*
Ohhh, my *GOD*, he just
Beats these men to *death*!"
That's part a' boxing, I want to sniff
You don't like that, you don't like boxing,
When in truth, watching men face
Smokin' Joe
Was more like Letterman, early on
When I was older
When he was putting random items
In a hydraulic press

Cosell (Co-Soul)*

Horseass Imitators
Run their mimicry
In imp simpering
Syllables of
Dog growl and peanut butter stick
(With a dash of nasal congestion)
Bald irony of any thwarted teacher's life:
Brilliance
Birthing
Ignorance
The masses are asses
But
You knew that

*--originally posted on jerryjazzmusician.com, 2/10

Give Me Mantle, Standing One-legged

The Metropolitans
That's their actual name
20th Century expansionism
Trying to be Abner Doubleday
Nodding, Father Time, at kids' kids' kids' kids
The N.Y. Metropolitans
Very Mudville, that name
"Casey" 'tache, dark wooden hanger
Gilded Age slang and flat cap
Strong, the way Choynski was strong
Charlie Mitchell and John L., Peter Jackson
Patina'd hard, still frightening through Taft
Respected as strolling greatness, Depression
Deathbed, must wheezes, Korean Conflict
And, it is The Space Age
And clowns have eyes rolling Vegas
Until a miracle no one saw coming,
Like the pipeline of farm system
Giving out, dark miracle, on the Yankees
And tradition, legacy, antiquity
Became just that, and The Pyramids
Rented lesser and aging, harmed might
Stand field, Round Table after Punic Wars
Lancelot's eye is not dimmed
He sees it
He gets it
New World, fun for horns blaring
As in, *OH! New World! Open the wrapper!*
Antiquity, though, knows
New worlds are Technicolor whitewash
You can call 'em Amazin'
You can call 'em Ray
If Mickey Mantle was immortal
There'd be no argument

Corporate's Head

Later on through the wormhole,
When a "FOX" that meant "*The Simpsons*"
Used to cancel anything not godlike after
Three weeks,
A notion that floated hope for a tick
Was something called, *Herman's Head*
The old Greek chorus, consisting of
3 people, dressed Stooge-triplet barbershop
"Uni", "Roy", and "Al"
These mugged and NERF-jibed
McCain puff-a-mump'd,
Popeyed "O"-mouths
Painlessly hacking one-liners
Punchlines with caffeine removed
As giants in an Earth soon Bizarro
Tanked up, backs turned
On oil treatment and gas treatment
Never heeding The Chorus,
Because as far back as the Hellenic
No one ever did,
And our trio of Lullaby-Lollipop Shills
Begat "hey, how 'bout…(snaps fingers) you
remember, in the 60s…?"
And their quadruplets floated hope, then
For a time
The old Greek chorus as vaudevillian
Still selling something
Still oily, lotsa gas

Sudden Death of Hope
(Super Bowl III, January 12th, 1969)

The rash boy, the brash one
The hippie-punk-hair thing-kid
His sneer was winning
3rd Quarter
He, They, It, The Future
Winning
It was time,
Baltimore fans, barely a murmur
Stood   joined hands
Mittens and gloves and bare hands
Cold, clammy, soft
Dry hands and rough
Doughy hands, those of sinew, of
"Take my hand," said one to another
A syncing began, unity undreamed
Shared intensity of Was,
The EverVoid opened
"They" began to emerge:
Berry, Ameche, Lenny Moore
Steve Myrha, L.G. Dupre, everyone
Iron as of Wholeness as Solid sky
1958, full weight
Plus Unitas, god, as when the world was new,
Gleam, Them, Power, Them, Dynamo of
The World That Then Was...
By the Jets water cooler,
Dark figure asks Joe Willie, once more,
"Well? You're gonna look like an idiot...*child*."
"I want it guaranteed," said Joe, staring,
Dry fear, at pantheon
"*Both knees*," said the figure, hot excitement
"Agreed," said Joe, tight
Two kinds of hope vanishing, instantly
Missing frames

Meanwhile, Across No Man's Land

Woman as Rolling Pin

It was always supposed to be
A Rockwell painting
Down market, low rent, it was
I've eaten pies from Brobdingnag
I've sat amid cardigans and DuMonts
Asbestos didn't hurt us and
Merthiolate cleansed my wounds
Tinsel to choke the atmosphere
At Christmas
The backslapping, OldBoyisms
Davy Crockett caps, still on their pegs
I walked these places, echo shoe
When priests still knelt
And nuns did likewise
But we weren't allowed to talk
About that latter
That was dirty

Woman as Fried

I imagine
If a human person's hurt
Enough
Maybe they come away
Avenger
Some third-tier fiction harpy
Or Bridget Fonda
As Karen Black Valentine as
Single White Human Devil Doll
But, more like, Haters justified
Behave good girl, because Death is
Only romantic
And Maximum Security
With actual, tilt-head succubi
Isn't even that;
Hell, Real?
Fine, let's argue
D'you wanta know?
I'm An Asshole, Girl! Your Pain is Fun!
KILL ME!!
Maybe I'll go see Satan   maybe
But you as Ruth Snyder, won't
#ZZZzzztttTTT!!#, Daily News,
Instead to a Hell undenied
Where murky, stygian
Tenebrous, darkling
Rayless, lightless is
The new, screaming Black

Woman as Stein

Refreshment, is grand
Otherness as chicken dinner, is
No, sorry, poor widdle, No!!
It's Grand
Otherness as a Kleenex, really is
Jesus Christ, do You have issues…
Usage is great, it's fun, it's POWER
It's grand,
The whole idea of Stepford is that,
If you can't be so depraved
Soulessness fulfills
Peter Bagge's "Lisa", screaming
Wannabe,
If crazed as euphoric insanity is
Not for you
Okay
Just shut your tears
'Cause this is grand
And, even if it's not
There can be no backannounced
"propriety"
Who the Hell, right mind, apologizes to
Drained Pilsner?

Woman as Lugosi

A haunted house leap from a closet of
"no"
As surprise birthday
For any dude ever thought he held an
Entitlement title
Claiming lifesblood
Claiming a Life
Claiming strength
A leap to plateau of
As Good As
Which makes them Same
Which makes them Men
Which fulfills the Gospel of Thomas
Or
Fulfills quip of de Beauvoir
Whether God or Realized Actual Other
though,
We won't know, 'til The War is Over
As all accepting, sweep up the
Dead

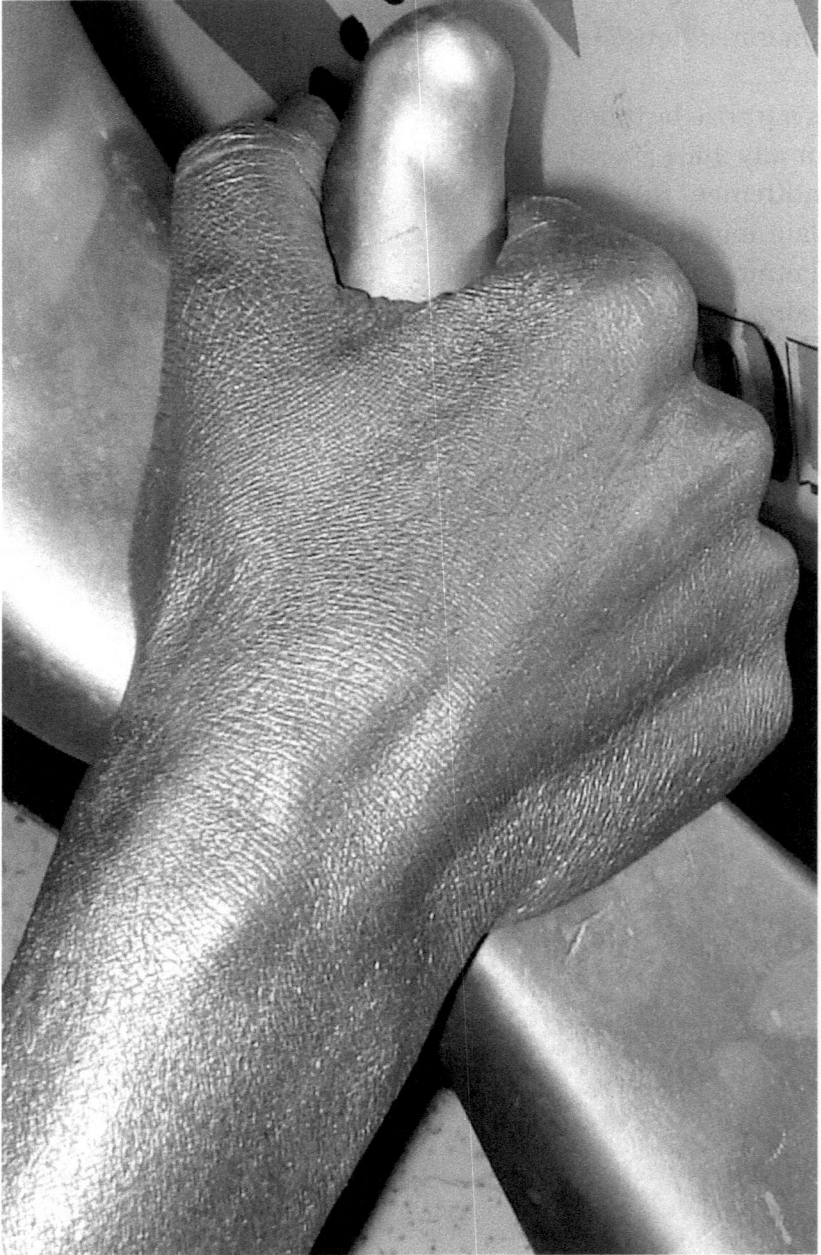

Woman as Rolling Stone

One dismisses established precedent
At one's own risk

Six Flag beerbottom clown glasses
Headband, mane restrained
(well, she should have washed it
she could be
a decent looking person
if she'd do something with herself)
Carole King wardrobe
Carly Simon mouth
A "what a mouth on her"
(it won't be like that
when I grow up)
I always thought of reassertion of
Right and Righteous
As Babi Yar for a good cause
So, cut to 11th grade, and I for the most
Spent vast majority,
Carter to Gingrich,
Sitting there with an invisible ledger
Ticking off dripping red marks
Mental gong, **"NO."**

One dismisses established precedent
One hopes for slingshot around the sun,
One shoots crap in Vegas
By way of Hollywood

Nuclear Family (final production year)

The whole reception was booze and
Sex jokes
That's pretty much Them, each and
Together
These are, got-the-grades
These are, did-Not-rebel
No fist for either reason
Late to postwar party, as caterers pack,
This yin and coupled yang, are a 'do'
A 'do' only and ever,
'Be' don't enter into it, Monty
Theirs', is willful limitation
'Cause yer dad HAS TUH
Beat ya up, every night!
Other-ize, how'd'ja grow up straight?
Visited to offspring, no matter suffering
Maturing, measuring nail depth x Cross
For, trial by fire
It will purge you, thus
Groom has taken in-like soft thing
Back to the cave
Turned it into a
Mechanical pincushion
And, this begat begetting
Which begat brood
Which begat domicile of
'Do', a do process of natural, normal
Which is a family
Judged by

It's Almost Midnight (Film at 11)

When Terror was only sinister*

It carried with it base cold
A chilliness of visage, the
Calculated iced hatred of a Fu Manchu
Some Soviet
One-eyed-guy-replete-with-patch-and-trademark-cheek-scar
Refrigerator Hatred, an "old" feeling
Courtesy of survivors of Eurasia's supercollision of
Ancient and Modern
But, with requisite maniacal laughter, natch
Just when They thought They had you;
When terror was sinister,
It was a poster
It was a character
It was a symbol
Now, it's an endless talking point
Hot milk for baby adults
Prayer in the fiery furnace discussions of
Children with whom I grew up,
Fanning the hammer, Cowboys and Injuns
Animated schoolyard confabbing, televised,
Revising Them
Reprising Rocket J. Squirrel

*--originally posted on jerryjazzmusician.com, 11/10

34

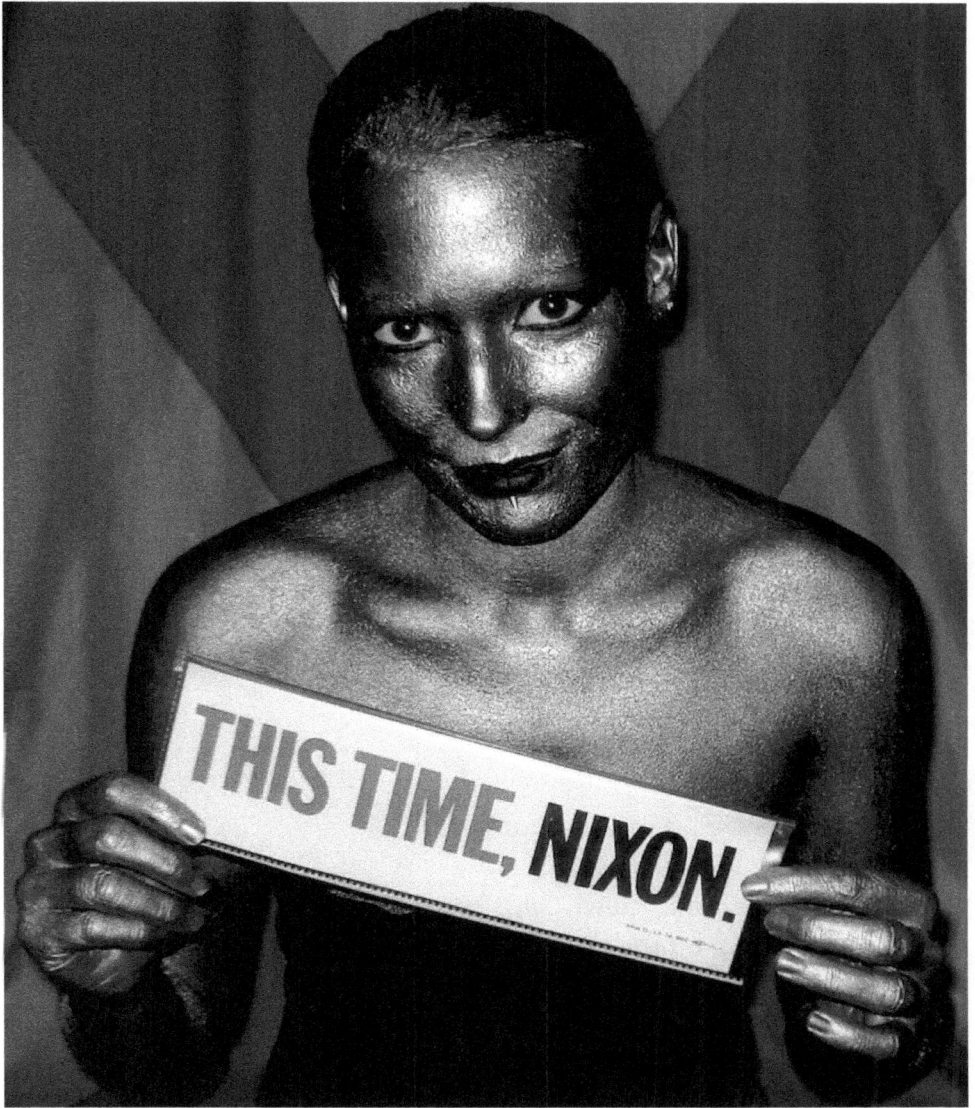

Lew-ten-naint Man

I remember myself in the cradle
Like all of you, I've line-itemed Freud,
So I, actual, recall Kennedy
With 'ee's chalk-talk
About "advisors"
Which never fools anyone
But, our government needs Cialis
Because short of Adolf Hitler
Wiping out half of Europe
Too many will believe divers peoples
Are entitled to be White Christian
Jeffersonian males
In their very own way;
My News on the March to *PLAYBOY*
Was ugly but annoying, a men's room
"Do I HAVE to look at that?"
Vietnam, was so no-soap at the Holiday Inn
In Alabama
With blood involved,
It was scream-cry rugby
It was nothing to do with Me
Until I turned 11, and stasis
And 12, and Dick'd said "honor", and
Stasis
And 13, stasis, and…now…whispers…
I never kept up on the news
Cronkite was nothing to do with Me
And, when Saigon fell, 'copters tumbling
I was 6' 1", silk shirt, 8th Grade
Thinkin' 'bout workin' on procreatin'
So, fact of "Lucky Man" by ELP
Not meaning more, now, than philosophy
Was a green light to a red light of

Beautiful music to m'testes
Saying, "just this"
Which never fools anyone

hoo-hoo-HOO!, Yestuhday's Tom Sawyahh...!
(w/apologies to Neal Peart)

Unsettling, faces wrapped in Red
Camou, dirtred
The damned air, mistred
When the choppers flew
Behind flak yakker reporting,
But national news, the kids who
Disobeyed
Bothered me way more
Mostly for running mouths,
I've run mine for ME, not for
Worldview A vs. Worldview B
Something apart, from the very first
"WHY DO YOU *CARE?!*"
If "humanity", okay, bless/dobbin/salaam
Let's begin with "yes, sir", "no, ma'am"
Respect of elders and the flag, manners
The Common Virtues, deportment
Proper place setting of your place
On the Food Chain
...oh, that's useless and stupid, huh?
Well, if sin is sin and selfishness is
Sociology 101
If wrong is wrong, harm is harm
Dehumanization is (okayokay)
Equal/equal, samey-same, s' all ONE
Okay   Then
You're all going to breaks rocks in Kansas
'Til you're 80
And while you're gone, we'll shake hands
Joke around, bury the hatchet, and
Tell all oppressed, maligned goodpeoples
We're sorry we were bad

You have my word
We'll pay for our sins, I swear it
Right after you've been processed

Shatnered Dreams
(Johnny Hates Contradiction)

Argosy, True, the *Police Gazette*
Love, Acceptance, buying the world a Coke,
Power
Unfulfillable longing,
Shakespearean strength
A sentinel's gentleness,
Protector, cue stick psycho
Protector, war poster tears,
Might of space opera, pulp era
Understanding his own, mortal future,
Steel greatness of blinding command
A god who makes no judgments At All

This, is what was once known
As destruction used as a form of creation
It was called "nuclear fission"
It birthed a whole, 'nuther world
One of Ahabs
Dicks
Wrath
And cons

I Am Not Pink

Leonard Nimoy
Can't sing at all
And therein lies the strength
Of his music

To The Rock Critic for the *New York Post*, re: "Space Oddity"

It's not that great a song
If you're no astronaut
Or never gave a rat's
About the space pogrom
If you can't relate to "leaving the girl behind",
Or if alienation isn't all that
Alien
To you
If Space is the unreal of *Trek* teatime,
If NASA is bullcrap between real news and
Sports
If you find hype legit
And individuals disposable,
If the idea of rebellion
(NOT involving Ben Franklin)
Makes you horribly honked
If the darkness of mere being
Is only upsetting if it's
YOURS
It's not too great a song,
Now, "Sledgehammer",
That's a great song
It's about sex

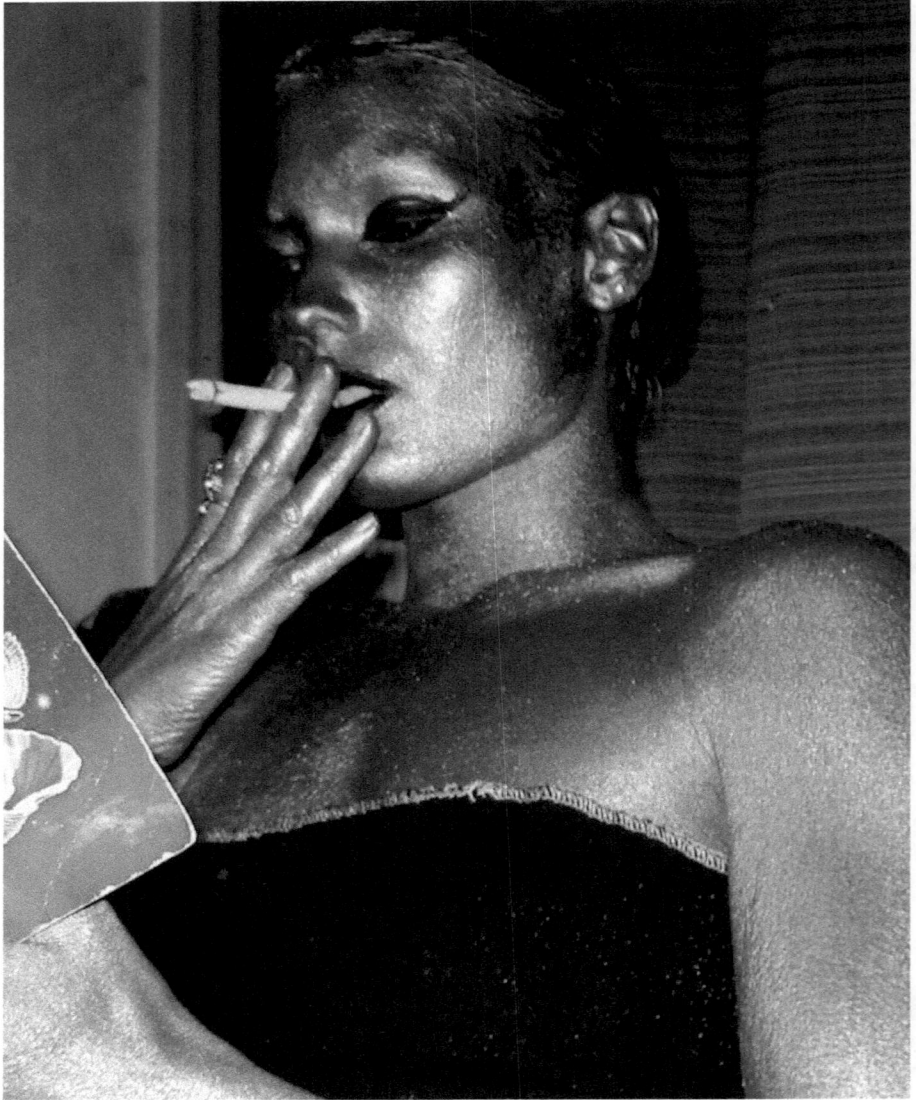

Thanks for the infinite recursive loop*

Mom, back when she still smoked
Hack-coughing, still laughing, parrot,
As Bob Hope's not funny, again
On *The Tonight Show*:
"Papua New Guinea, ladies and gentlemen!
Papua and *New Guinea!*
Ain't nothin' "new" in New Guinea,
Way down yonder in the Papua patch!"
Color-bled people, many dead for ages,
Baa-ing woolly delight at
Saccharine Old Show Biz,
Noses tunneling up, into their faces
As my geekazoid bud shows me the graphic he made,
OTEP, full frontal
Doing a slow, SEGA 16-bit softshoe
Back and forth across the screen,
"Look, I can put Git-Mo behind her!
She's strutting it in front of Git-Mo!"
And all I hear is filtered smoke
And all I see are sheep cries,
As Johnny tells karma We'll Be Right Back

*--originally posted on jerryjazzmusician.com, 11/10

Your hands. My perspective.
(click clack)

On the way to school
Another kid showed me
Klackers, KlickKlacks, Quick Klack,
I didn't even want 'em
But they looked cool
Clackers, ClickClacks, Ker Knockers,
Beloved dime store keeping up with the
Times
Mom bitch-shelled, and
Popper Knockers, KlikKlak Bonkers
Clackers ClackClacks ClickClacks
The logistics meant no more to a
Pre-Asperger's Aspergian
(*grrreat*, a Diff-EQ Duncan yo-yo)
Crackers K-Nokkers Ker-Knockers
Because the trouble with men (even as boys)
One has to hang in there after Oops, mistake
Klackers Klick Klacks Knockers Mini Poppers
Follow after, and if no good at predetermined
Follow After
Moon Rocks PopperKnockers Rockers
Super Clackers QuickKlacks QuickClacks
Entitlement issues? Not't'tall
I don't want acrylic chips in my eyes
I don't want to lead, either
And, you're not the congenital idiot of Me,
QuickWacks Wackers   Whackers
Fine, let's fight
As bolas, these of old were weapons,
Yes, I'm 8, I get it, I'll go to juvie
But, you wanta tribe me, Golding
Give my Aunt who died of cancer
My Love
Whak KOs

46

Closing Arguments for the Defense

they were

Our liquored neighbor across the street,
The retired dentist, who gave us gum,
My mother's crass friend and her husband,
The school principal who looked like
He'd been in Harding's cabinet,
The old man who sold his building to Dad
Crammed with confectionery machines,
The crabby woman a block away
Yelling a strange term at me, "leash laws",
The Monsignor who baptized me,
The elderly lady in the mansion two doors down,
My 3rd grade teacher, who by the time I hit 4th
I heard, was in a nursing home,
There aren't enough books to list them
There aren't enough books
Unless the Book of Revelation is true
And also accurate, when it uses the term,
"books",
This partial list, is most of the reason
Why I sat it out,
"Life's too short!", you mockingbirds screech,
Yes   I Know That
Fuck it
That's too much pressure to even begin
To try to have a good time

Mercer University, Coop TV Room, 11/80

Just a few, us guys
Actual *Trek,* before the bullshit
It was the "Methusaleh" one
The one with the one good, chilling,
"I…am Brahms…"
Hurr…! HurrHurr, HurrHurr…!
The rest, I didn't catch, 'til my 30s
So, at 19, there I was, watching Kirk fight
Sad the one good,
I-Love-Ancient-Plot-Themes
Was over
And, the overdressed android chick
Spouts a nursery school version
Of a current Reality I hide in my home
To avoid
And, I watch her posture, Romper Room
Intense, thinking,
Hurr…! HurrHurr, HurrHurr…!
About a taste of dust, and
Android Ding Dong School
Tastes the floor
And the TV room, with so few of us
Receives dramatic silence of
It's-3rd-Season-We're-Done-For
And I, predating
MST 3000's debut by 8 years,
I intone,
"Because he didn't use Ray-O-Vac."
HUGE LAUGH
(mental end zone dance)
I tended not to share that, on dates

The Track Not Hidden
(Midway's Golden Arm, Far Right Score)

For You, it's been a lifetime;
For Me, it's been an hour

Graduate school concepts of "appropriate"
Only ever turn those counseled
Into witch hunters
Villages require perpetual motion failsafe
An engine of center,
Anti-motivation of What-Happens-IF
This can be The Law
It can be YHWH
It can be humanistic principle
It can't be B.F. Skinner
Too many mud-people
Are Cain and tribe, into the world
A phrase I heard a friend use, once,
"the final collapse, the tear jerker"
Gives way to a phrase you've heard,
"bottoming out"
And, not to be Hunter S. about it, but
20, 40, 60 miles from you, reading
There is a room, a place,
A darkened space sparse of furniture
Where Neanderthal, unrepentant,
Watches skin colors change, somatic death
Of Cro-Magnon
Worried hollow Only of steel carbon bars;
There is no dark, burning Wonka blessing
Hela-Hades Golden Ticket
As Cap's shield against incarceration
And, though far counties from The Box,
I do understand that...The center holds...
I make no further promises...
That primitive, can be Oppenheimer, but

It understands a different understanding
I don't understand Eastwood's
"orangutan" movies
I understand *Unforgiven*

Roberto

Whatever dreams were mine in 1969, I was screamed from into waking, 1/1/70. My buddy had the television on. Everything was advertisements, wild colors and fonts *ala* Peter Max. Familiar Welk voices instead pumped wild, *"THE 70s ARE HERE...!!"* What passed then, for color gels. Old people fast for Young as their 'look', Youth grinning patronizing, behind masks. New ideas, New TV shows, New everything! Ads for upcoming, HERE, right NOW, headed *this way*, singing, dancing, Fun*FUN*fuhfuh-*fun*, mid-movie Community dance in *Oliver Twist*, but Young and Here and Now (corporate), as Joseph Cotten delivered silvered lines in mindseye, *"Old times aren't new, they're* dead!*"*, and Welles pumped the sound until all I knew was, long years before the song, "What A Difference A Day Makes", TV as BFF, had turned. Loud (corporate) grin of HappyYouth, VitalWild, it said my world was dead. At least, like a kid's missing grandparent, it had gone away on a trip. The strong-arm press, and not hidden, for "change your mind this instant!", light switch, was palpable. Years later, I'd read this shit as Orwell. *Whonk-Whonk*, went the Peace Train! Get on Board!

The TV was a music box, that day, explosions of "DIFFERENT!!", "CHANGED!!", "NEW!!"...and this, I knew, to be over-the-top indeed. Silliness. Goofiness. Camp. The *#BIFF#*, *#ZAM#*, *#POW#* of Batman and Robin. Entertainment. Nothing more. Nothing to be gleaned, no wisdom, not allowed--but, *goddam*, it was LOUD! Pushed at 90 miles an hour. As if feet had set again upon the Mount of Olives, if we'd just listen (corporate) and follow instructions. I found the barrage, irritating. Making but one mental note per *Nanny and the Professor*, I was relieved when Mom showed up. I never asked about her penny poker or loud laughs, btw. In the place where I'd fallen asleep, you kept yourself to yourself.

Cut to summer, baseball season. Lots of "Mets" talk, Tom Seaver buzz. I'd begun collecting cards, the previous year; I liked the idea of ownership, Joe Citizen in the making. But, after a summer jaunt for wax packs, the sobering counterpoint, at last:

Lucky little man, I early scored a Clemente. The name star had been with Pittsburgh, from The Cold War. America, Then, Ellis Island'd his Christian name (for public consumption), to "Bob". I didn't know social politics or power relationships. I knew the Bucs had a helluva player, name of "Bob Clemente". Until 1970.

The great man, scant years before tragedy, was archival **Yes, We Can!** about his angle and tilt of head. His visage, no-nonsense from memory, was to the sky, and far. His name? Very different. Not chewing gum. Not Gillette fights. Not double-breasted. Not hard drinking men, forcing and straining at dime-games of chance. No pulleys, tension-weight or simple machines as thralls of Man. No beer or smoke wafts, atmosphere. No Mom and Dad and Junior, Jesus behind them, flag up above. Not flat or simple or primitive or 'the same'. The 1970 TOPPS of the Pittsburgh Pirates' claim to fame, showed a man named, "*Roberto* Clemente"... and, indeed, that's the name I heard from then, on. When, much later, as I aged, the Original Reality got referenced at all, it bore the Scarlet "N/A". *Oops, mistake. We're a loving people, a good people. We're a decent country, a nice country. That was Then, this is Now. Pay no attention, to that history behind the screen.*

But...that was it. Period. My world otherwise, continued same. Peaceful, in the personal. Beyond my eyes, a rioting brotherhood, banging out Tom Lehrer against skulls. The white folks hated the black folks and the black folks hated the white folks. The rich folks hated the poor folks and the poor folks hated the rich folks. The President hated the students and the students hated him, and the American Nazis just hated, and everyone hated Vietnam. As Heston as Moses, I looked around my quiet corner, at salesmen's smiles and theater marquees, soda machines and children in my class. Our desks, Kennedy. The teachers, Hoover. The building, McKinley. My city, Marquette and Joliet, guided Indian canoe. "6" or "7", it was still America. The same mortar, same mortar and pestle, same mores that were ours, the year before. Barbershop poles, perpetual spin, as waiting denizens warred, reflex, scoring with the sound of a watch, wound. Bars echoing with XY community, muscle and maintaining, on-tap quaffs and arm wrestling. Bowling alleys, crash of pins to take the frame, quilted team jackets, chemical cleansing, competition against a robot arm. The annual fair, sugar-food smells and mustard meat, some eternal, bawling kid nearby, Gore-hot under tent as braggarts and wannabe's fought The Immovable, Golden Object. Solidity. Permanency. Normalcy. What change is there, in Us?

Nada, nonfriend. Nothing changed. Nothing but that name. And this was key, as the name spoke The Future. Not because we'd reached It. Because we were told we didn't have a choice. Three Card Monte, laced with doubleplusbullshit. The prod. The nudge. The "gaslight". The Jedi media trick, "education" trick, indoctrination trick, the shepherding of immense Herd, by a few...worse, the "going along with", the nod, the agreement, the concession, the genuflection. And, to call this not only right and righteous, but for men to bare chest, teeth, to Wendigo-bellow--then claim *conformity, sameness,* makes a "man"—then, to say *You* made that decision? Very reminiscent, I'd say, of a dear friend of yore, mocking early PC: "C'mon and join the Nonconformist-Conformist Movement, 'where being The Same, makes a difference'!" A laugh and a half. Until you think about the message.

The secret to Midway's Golden Arm, now 100-button control of 4D Kill-Die is the male bonding of the day, I feel I can safely relate. You don't push evenly. You don't strain gradually. You don't take on the mute arm, *mano-a-mano*, fair fight. The

56

tension is set, so to prevent more than a moderate score, even if you once played Lurch or starred in *Moonraker*. The "win", all the way and easy, to be crowned with "belonging in a zoo", is not a test of strength, at all. It's speed, Mickey. Greasy-fast. Quick whip, Daniel at ice, nothing but reflex. Ali's joke, about "wanna see it, again?" You'll triumph, every time. And belong in a zoo. As will everyone paying attention. Because monkey see, monkey do—right? Whether American ingenuity, 1969, or Jedi (corporate), 1970, it's really B.F. Skinner, 1938. And that, I think, is the crime.

Nonfriend, until you concede even The Scientific Method is structured, Amway chart, to produce outcome-as-ordered, don't you dare slam the door on those earnest, plain-looking ladies, or on the young men in white shirts and ties. And, buy magazine deals from every solicitor. Those kids have to walk a long way.

—CEE, 7/12/14

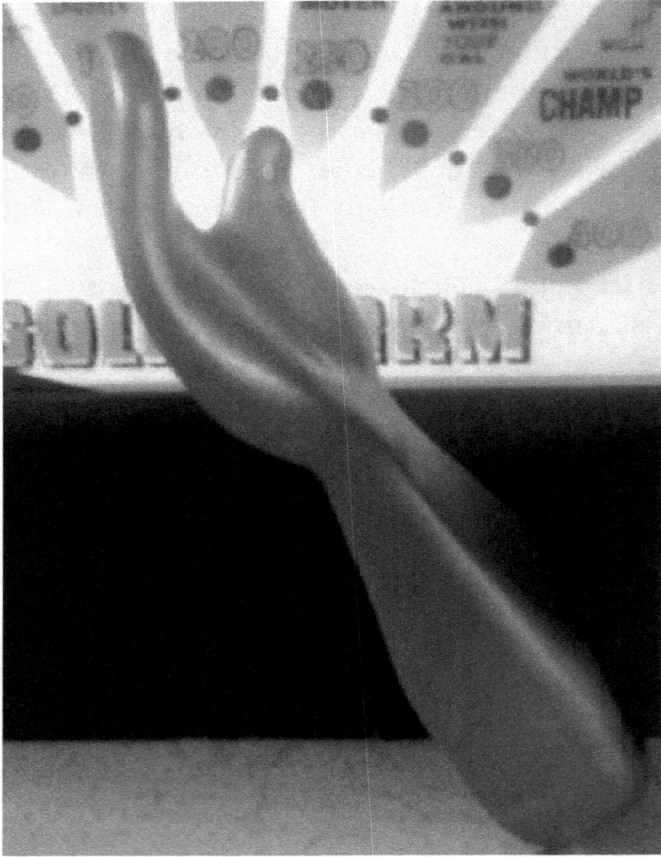

"Here, is only a graveyard, Denny. Get out of here, do not look back. Here is only dead things."

—from the final voice-over from the
CEE screenplay series,
Somehow, I Still Believe

www.ingramcontent.com/pod-product-compliance
Lightning Source LLC
Chambersburg PA
CBHW060722030426
42337CB00017B/2965